FLASHCARD BOOKS

NUMBERS
SHAPES & COLORS

ENGLISH

to

JAPANESE

FLASHCARD BOOK

BLACK & WHITE EDITION

HOW TO USE:

- READ THE ENGLISH WORD ON THE FIRST PAGE.

- IF YOU KNOW THE TRANSLATION SAY IT OUT LOUD.

- TURN THE PAGE AND SEE IF YOU GOT IT RIGHT.

- IF YOU GUESSED CORRECTLY, WELL DONE!
IF NOT, TRY READING THE WORD USING THE PHONETIC PRONUNCIATION GUIDE.

- NOW TRY THE NEXT PAGE.
THE MORE YOU PRACTICE THE BETTER YOU WILL GET!

BOOKS IN THIS SERIES:
ANIMALS
NUMBERS SHAPES AND COLORS
HOUSEHOLD ITEMS
CLOTHES

ALSO AVAILABLE IN OTHER LANGUAGES INCLUDING:

FRENCH, GERMAN, SPANISH, ITALIAN,

RUSSIAN, CHINESE, JAPANESE AND MORE.

WWW.FLASHCARDEBOOKS.COM

One

いち

Ichi

Two

2

に

Ni

Three

さん

San

Four

し／よん

Shi/ Yon

Five

ジ

Go

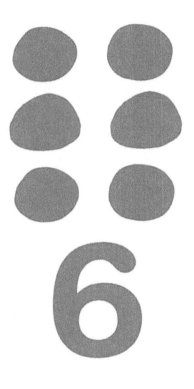

Six

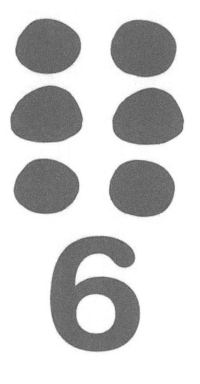

6

ろく

Roku

Seven

しち／なな

Shichi/ Nana

Eight

はち

Hachi

Nine

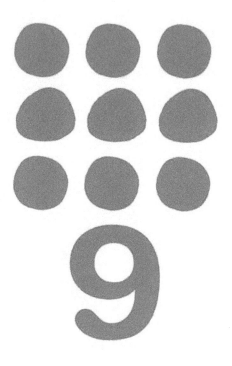

く／きゅう

Ku/ Kyuu

Ten

じゅう

Juu

Eleven

11

じゅういち

Juuichi

Twelve

12

じゅうに

Juuni

Thirteen

じゅうさん

Juusan

Fourteen

14

じゅうし／じゅうよん

Juusi/ Juuyon

Fifteen

じゅうご

Juugo

Sixteen

16

じゅうろく

Juuroku

Seventeen

じゅうしち／じゅうなな

Juushichi/ Juunana

Eighteen

じゅうはち

Juuhachi

Nineteen

19

じゅうく／じゅうきゅう

Juuku/ Juukyuu

Twenty

20

にじゅう

Nijuu

30

Thirty

30

さんじゅう

Sanjuu

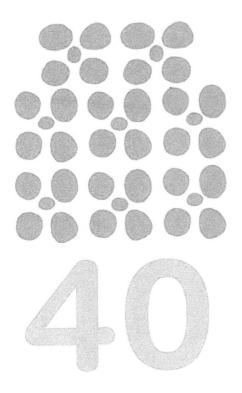

Forty

40

よんじゅう

Yonjuu

50

Fifty

50

ごじゅう

Gojuu

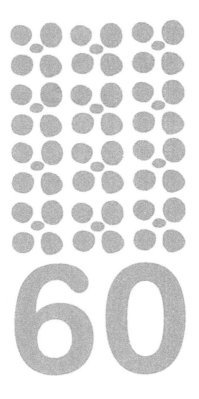

Sixty

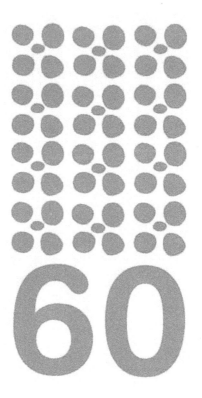

60

ろくじゅう

Rokujuu

Seventy

70

ななじゅう

Nanajuu

Eighty

80

はちじゅう

Hachijuu

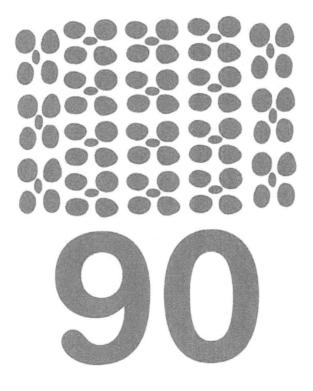

Ninety

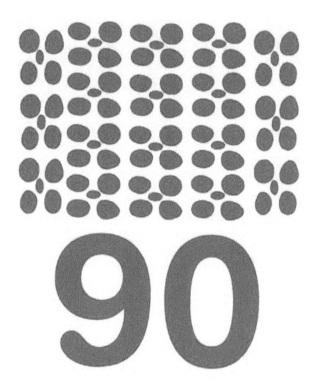

90

きゅうじゅう

Kyuujuu

100

One Hundred

100

ひゃく

Hyaku

1,000

One thousand

1,000

せん

Sen

1,000,000

One Million

1,000,000

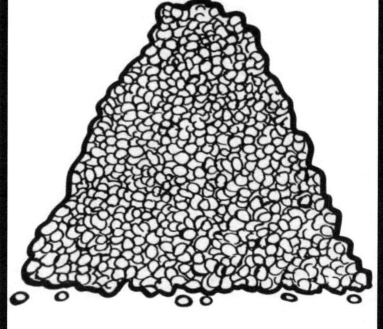

ひゃくまん

Hyakuman

Red

あか

Aka

Yellow

きいろ

Kiiro

Pink

ぴんく

Pinku

Blue

あお

Ao

Black

くろ

Kuro

White

しろ

Shiro

Brown

ちゃいろ

Chairo

Green

みどり

Midori

Orange

おれんじ

Orenji

Grey

はいいろ

Haiiro

Purple

むらさき

Murasaki

Square

しかく／せいほうけい

Shikaku/Seihoukei

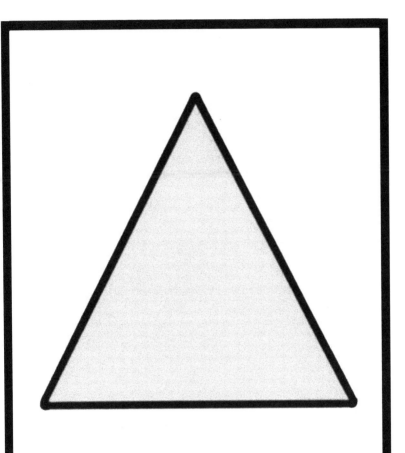

Triangle

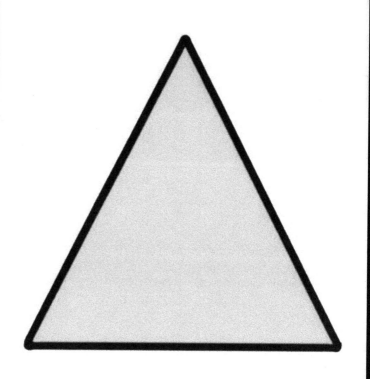

さんかく／さんかくけい

Sankaku/Sankakukei

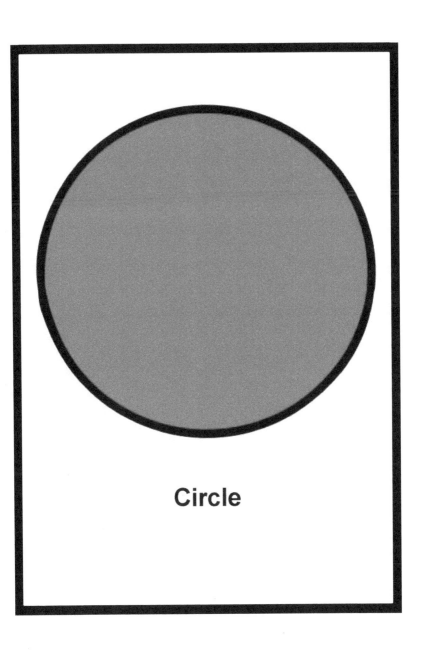

Circle

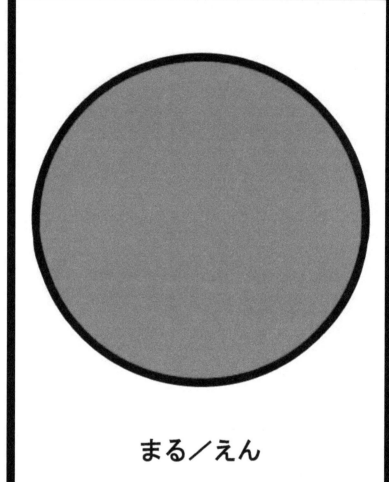

まる／えん

Maru/En

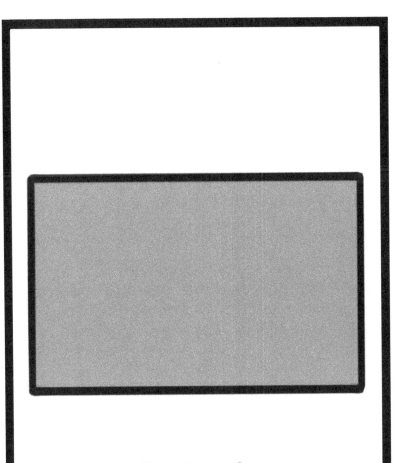

Rectangle

ちょうほうけい

Chouhoukei

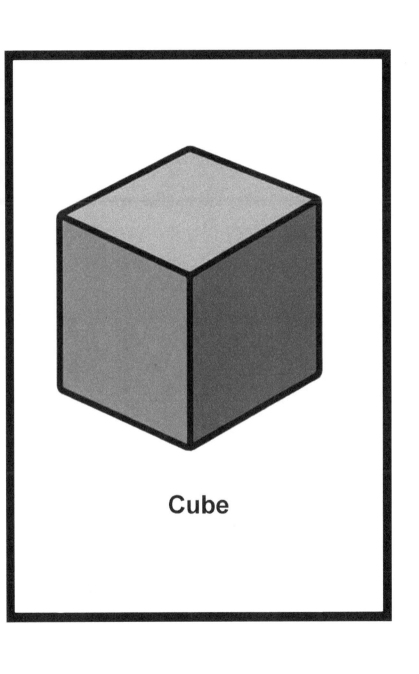

Cube

りっぽうたい

Rippoutai

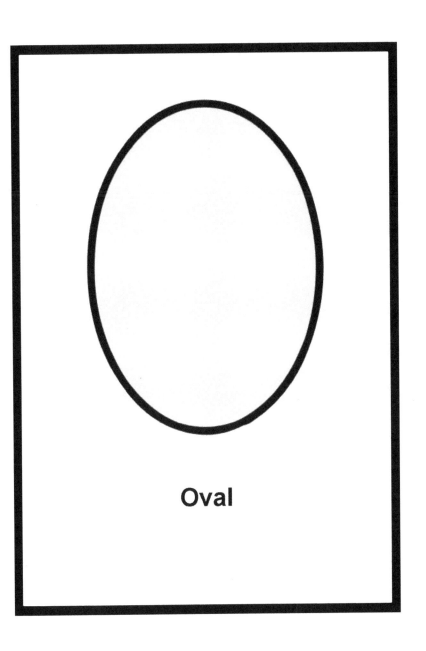

Oval

だえんけい

Daenkei

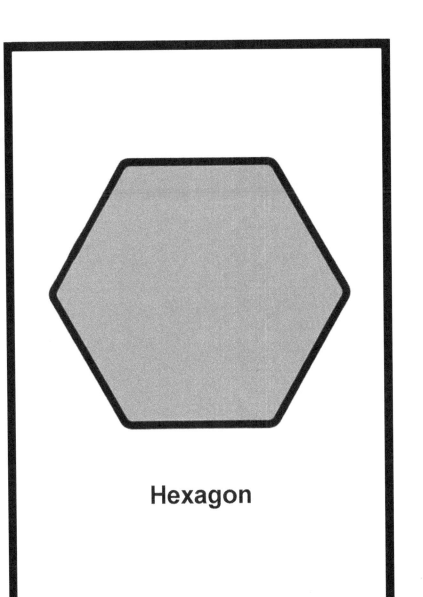

Hexagon

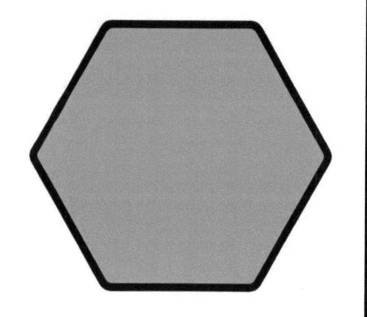

ろっかくけい

Rokkakukei

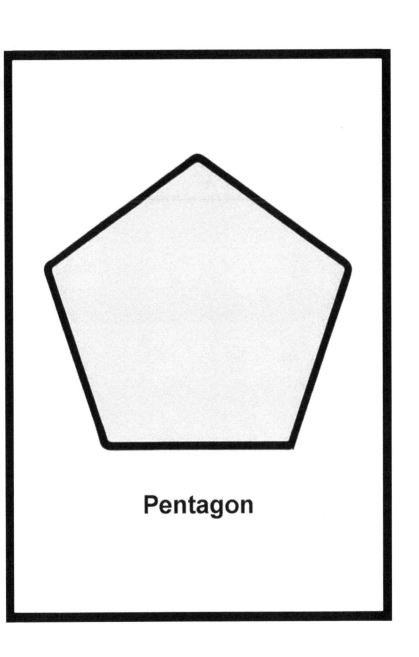

Pentagon

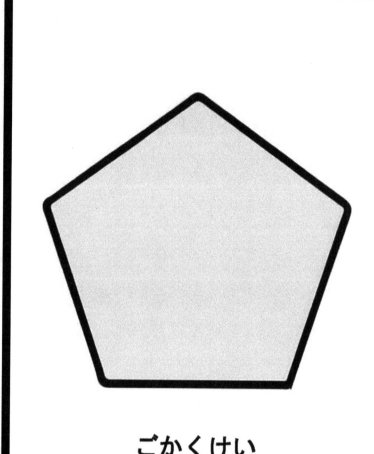

ごかくけい

Gokakukei

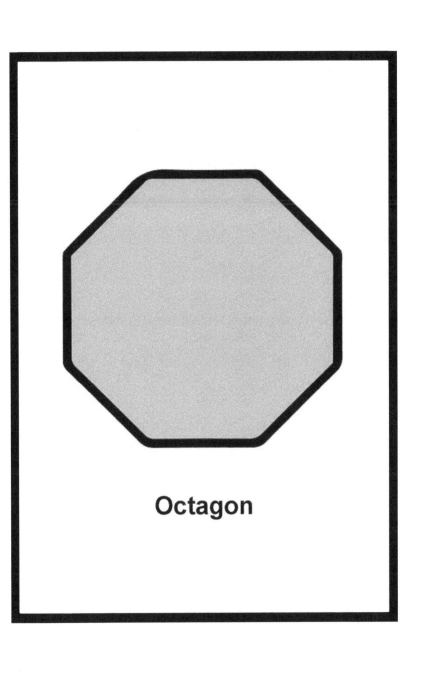

Octagon

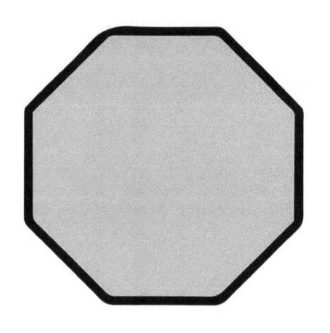

はっかくけい

Hakkakukei

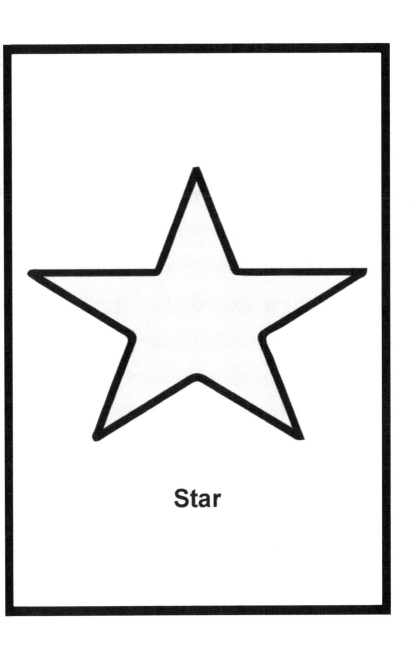

Star

ほし

Hoshi

Heart

はーと

Ha-to

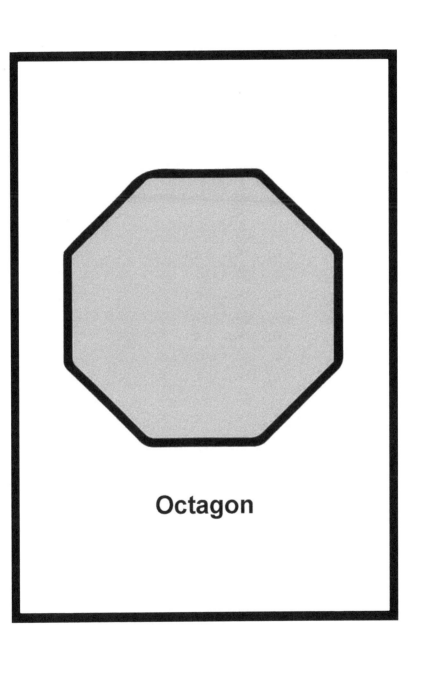

Octagon

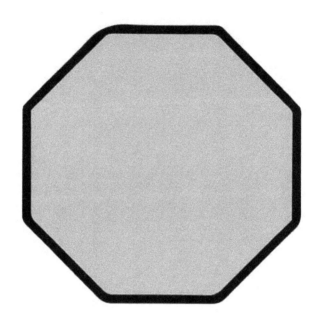

はっかくけい

Hakkakukei

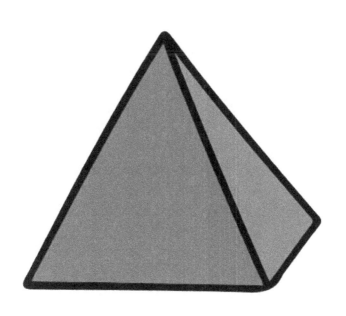

Pyramid

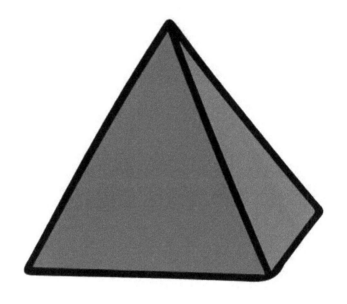

かくすい

Kakusui

Cylinder

えんちゅう

Enchuu

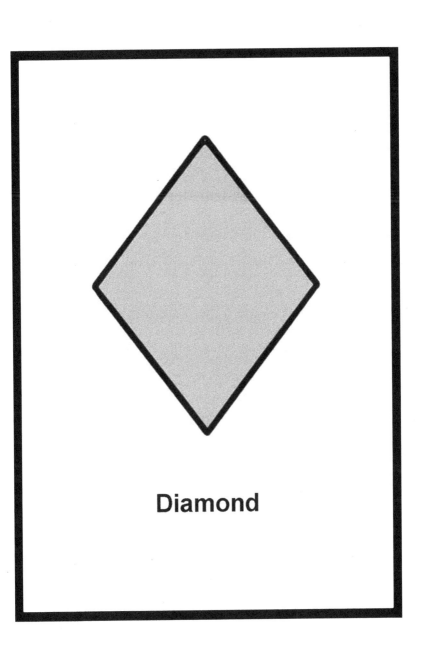

Diamond

ひしがた

Hishigata

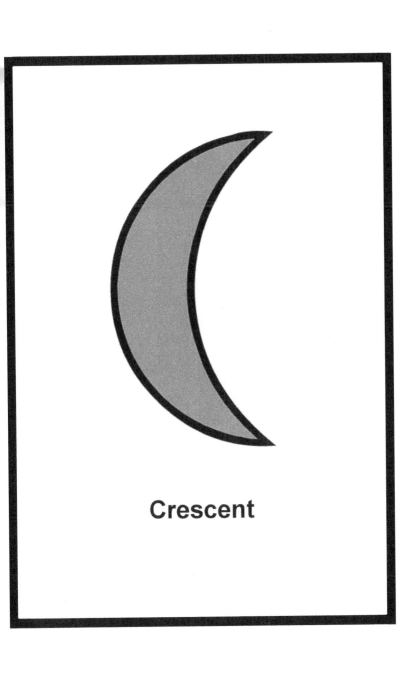

Crescent

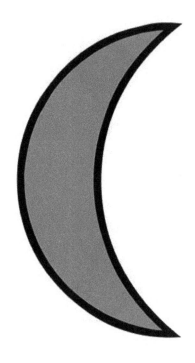

みかづき

Mikazuki

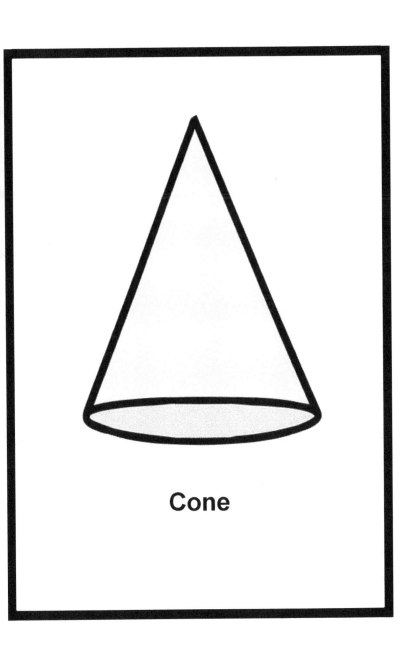

Cone

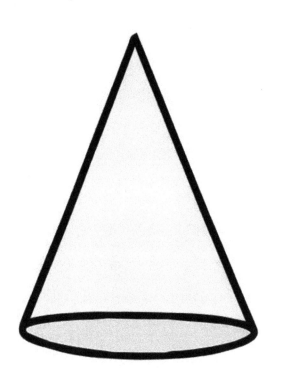

えんすい

Ensui

CPSIA information can be obtained
at www.ICGtesting.com
Printed in the USA
FSHW012002050819
60761FS